TELEPHONE
JOKES

By Katy Hall and Lisa Eisenberg
Illustrated by John DeVore

SCHOLASTIC INC.
New York Toronto London Auckland Sydney

For Andrew Zebell!

No part of this publication may be reproduced in whole or in part, or stored in a retrieval system, or transmitted in any form or by any means, electronic, mechanical, photocopying, recording, or otherwise, without written permission of the publisher. For information regarding permission, write to Scholastic Inc., 555 Broadway, New York, NY 10012.

ISBN 0-590-48575-X

12   8 9/9

Printed in the U.S.A.   01

First Scholastic printing, October 1994

What is the cheapest time to call your friends long distance?

When they're not home!

When doesn't a telephone work under-
water?

When it's wringing wet!

What do you get when you cross a telephone with a pair of pants?

Bell-*bottoms!*

How can you tell if a bee is on the phone?

You get a buzzy signal.

What do you call a large person who constantly calls up people, pretending to be somebody else?

A big phone-y!

Irv: Can you telephone from the space shuttle?

Marv: Of course I can *tell a phone* from the space shuttle! The phone's the one with the long cord!

PHONE BOOKS YOU HOPE YOU NEVER OPEN!

How to Avoid Long Phone Calls
by Xavier Breath

Can You Dial Direct?
by Fred I. Kant

Is This Phone Call Over?
by Midas Wellby

Calling the Barnyard
by Tobias A. Pigg

Midnight Phone Calls
by Eliza Wake Now

TELE-(PHONE)-VISION

9:00   *Saved by the Phone Bell*

10:00   *Sesa-it's-for-me! Street*

11:00   Movie of the Week: *The Call-Waiting of the Wild*

12:00   Movie of the Month: *He's Not Home Alone Right Now, II*

1:00   Cartoon: *Chip 'n Dial Rescue Rangers*

2:00   *Life-dials of the Rich and Famous*

3:00   *Lambchop's Play-a-long Distance*

4:00   *Read-ding-a-ling-a-ling Rainbow*

5:00 *Rom-per-son-to-person Room*

6:00 *Nightly Busy-ness Report*

7:00 *Fresh Prince of Bell-Air*

8:00 *Phe-wrong-nom-ber*

9:00 *Saturday Night Live Wire*

10:00 *Hangin' Up on Mr. Cooper*

Bob's phone rang in the middle of the night.

"Hello?" he said.

"Hello," said a voice. "Is this Tommy?"

"No," said Bob. "You must have the wrong number."

"Oh, sorry," said the caller. "I hope I didn't wake you."

"Oh, that's okay," said Bob. "I had to get up anyway, to answer the phone!"

TELEPHONE RING RINGS

Ring, ring!
Who's there?
Dial!
Dial who?
Dial come to the phone as soon as her
  sister, Bea, gets off!

Ring, ring!
Who's there?
Operator!
Operator who?
Operator peanut butter sandwich too
   fast, and now she can't talk!

Tammy: What are you doing, Tim?

Tim: I'm trying to call Washington!

Tammy: Oh, haven't you heard? He's dead!

Tim: Tammy, who was that on the phone?

Tammy: Oh, just a woman saying it was long distance from China. But I told her I already knew that!

TELEPHONE CALLS YOU HOPE YOU'LL NEVER GET!

Party Host: Hello?

Phone Caller: I'm trying to reach a Ms. Nidiot. Her first name is Ima. Could you please ask if anybody at your party knows her?

Party Host: I'd be glad to. Please hold on. *(yells)* Excuse me, but does anybody know Ima Nidiot?

Party Host: Hello?

Phone Caller: Hello. I'm trying to reach a Mr. Yuppyernose. He goes by his initials I.C. Would it be too much trouble for you to ask your guests if any of them know him?

Party Host: Not at all. Hold the line please. *(yells)* Hey, everybody! Do any of you know I.C. Yuppyernose?

Party Host: Hello?

Phone Caller: Hello! I'm trying to reach a Ms. Leavinsoon. Her first name is Yula Bea? Could you find out if anybody at your party knows her?

Party Host: Hey, everybody! Do any of you know Yula Bea Leavinsoon?

Party Guests: 'Bye!

Caller: Operator! Operator! Do you know my boyfriend's line has been busy for an hour?

Operator: No, but if you hum a few bars, I might be able to sing along with you.

Caller: Operator! Operator! Call me an ambulance!

Operator: Okay. You're an ambulance!

Caller: Operator! Operator! I don't know what's wrong with my phone, but I can't make long distance calls any longer!

Operator: Don't worry. Your long distance calls are long enough already!

Caller: Operator! Operator! What's the fastest way for me to get to the hospital?

Operator: Have you tried playing in traffic?

PHONE NUMBERS
WE'D LIKE TO SEE

To call up a scuba diver, just dial . . .

1-800-H20

To call up a star baseball player, just dial . . .

1-800-RBI

ANSWER THE PHONE!

Answer: Area code!
Question: What do you call the secret
language used in your area?

Answer: Phone bill!
Question: What should you do when you want to talk to Bill?

Answer: Long distance!
Question: What's the best way to talk to King Kong?

RING-A-DING DINGERS

Lady: Hello, police? Please send an officer over to 324 Pine Street right away!

Hal: Sorry, this isn't the police station. It's Hal's Delicatessen.

Lady: Oh. Well, in that case, please send over a pastrami sandwich!

Dan: Hello? What's up?
Fran: The price of a burger!

Estelle: Hello?

Shirley: Hello! Boy, have I got some really juicy gossip for you, Laverne.

Estelle: I'm sorry, this isn't Laverne. You must have the wrong number. But anyway, what's the gossip?

Mr. Swanson: Hello? This is Mr. Swanson. Is this the butcher?
Butcher: Yup. Glad to meat you!

Bunny: Hello, honey? How about a date?

Honey: You want a date? Okay! How's 1066 B.C.?

Bob: Hello? I'm not interrupting your dinner, am I?

Rob: Actually, you are.

Bob: Good. Wait for me, and I'll be right over!

OPERATOR, OPERATOR

Caller: Operator! Operator! Can you hear me? I'm hiding under my bed-spread so my parents can't hear me.
Operator: Hmmm. Sounds like a cover-up to me!

Caller: Operator! Operator! Can you understand me? I'm chewing on a pancake while I talk to you.

Operator: Oh, how waffle!

Caller: My goodness, Operator! Your nose is so stuffed up, I can't understand you. You should really take something for that cold.

Operator: Good idea. I'll take the rest of the day off!

ANIMAL LINES

What animals talk on the telephone the most?

The yakety-yaks!

Caller: Finally! I got through! I've been trying to call the zoo for hours!

Zookeeper: Yes, all our lions were busy!

HELP! THE LINES
ARE CROSSED!

What do you get if you cross your telephone with a tape recorder and an alligator?

A snappy answering machine!

What do you get if you cross a phone with a rooster?

A wake-up call!

What do you get if you cross a wake-up call with a chicken?

An alarm cluck!

Caller: Operator! Operator! I need you to connect me with someone in my diet support group! I feel hungry but I don't want to eat!

Operator: I was hungry, too, but after talking to you, I'm fed up!

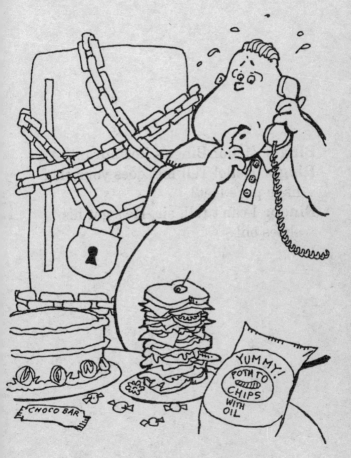

HELLO?
BINGO'S RESTAURANT!

Bingo: Hello? Bingo's Restaurant.
Ringo: Hello! Tell me, does your chef have pig's feet?
Bingo: I can't tell, sir. He's got his shoes on!

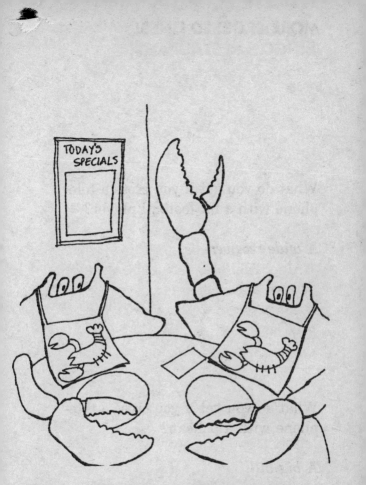

Bingo: Hello? Bingo's Restaurant.

Ringo: Hello! I'd like to know, do you serve crabs?

Bingo: We serve anyone, sir! Come on in!

What do you get if you cross a telephone with a fat football player?

A wide receiver.

What do you get if you cross a telephone with a pelican?

A big bill.

What do you get if you cross a telephone with a night crawler?

Ringworm!

What do you get if you cross a telephone with a vacuum cleaner?

We don't know what to call it, just don't put it close to your ear!

ANSWER THE PHONE — AGAIN!

Answer: Hello? Hello? Hello?
Question: How does a three-headed secretary answer the phone?

Answer: Dial soap.
Question: How do you stop dirty phone calls?

Answer: Himalayan.
Question: In what position is a boy while he talks on the phone?

How do angels answer the phone?

Halo?

How do molded fruit-flavored desserts answer the phone?

Jell-O?

How do scaredy-cats answer the phone?

Yellow?

How do, like, really laid-back types
answer the phone?

Mellow.

BEASTLY PHONE CALLS!

Why did the chicken walk on the telephone wire?

She wanted to lay it on the line!

How do little rattlesnakes call home?

Poison-to-poison.

Why do squirrels like to sit on telephone poles?

To stay away from the nuts on the ground!

Why didn't the skeleton need a telephone?

He had no body to talk with!

Why didn't the mummy want a telephone?

He always got too wrapped up in his calls!

Why did the vampire answer the phone in his pajamas?

He couldn't find his bat robe!

HOT CROSSED LINES!

What do you get if you cross a broken telephone with a football player?

A quarterback.

What do you get if you cross a telephone with a ghost?

A phantom caller!

What do you get if you cross a telephone with a hunting dog?

A golden receiver!

PHONE MANNERS

What did the cannibal mother say to the cannibal child when he was talking on the phone at dinnertime?

"How many times have I told you not to talk with someone in your mouth?"

What is the proper thing for me to say to a big ugly troll who's talking on two phones at the same time?

Say anything you want — he can't hear you!

PHONE WORLD! PHONE WORLD! PHONE WORLD!

How is a telephone like a dirty bathtub?

They both have rings!

What did the answering machine say to
the telephone?

Take my word for it.

What did the fax machine say to the
telephone?

You send me!

What did the pay phone say when the
quarter got stuck inside it?

Money's tight these days!

Why couldn't the skunk use her phone?

It was out of odor.

How does a cheerleader answer the phone?

Y–E–L–L–O!

How does a lobster answer the phone?

Shello?

How does a door chime answer the phone?

Bello?

BUSY SIGNALS

How can you tell if someone who's just had a perm is on the phone?

You get a frizzy signal!

How can you tell if someone who's having a temper tantrum is on the phone?

You get a tizzy signal!

EVEN <u>MORE</u> CROSSED LINES!

What do you get if you cross a telephone with an Italian dinner?

Spaghetti and meat bells!

What do you get if you cross a telephone with an iron?

A smooth operator!

What do you get if you cross a telephone with a vampire?

A ring-a-ding ding bat!

BABY BELLS

What did the little phone want to do
when she grew up?

Join Ringling Brothers Circus!

What did the proud telephone couple name their new quadruplets?

Annabelle, Arline, Cordelia, and Jack.

What happened to the little frog who
sat on the telephone?

He grew up to be a bellhop!

Why did Mrs. Yak call Mrs. Gnu after she'd just had twins?

To yak about the latest gnus.

When does a horse talk on the phone?

Whinny wants to!

What does a polar bear operator say?

"Glad I cold help you. Have an ice day!"

How does a football player make phone calls?

On a touch-down phone.

How does a baritone make phone calls?

Song distance!

How does Ebenezer Scrooge make phone calls?

Collect!

What do you get if you cross a phone
with a birthday celebration?

A party line!

What do you get if you cross a phone with a pair of glasses?

A television.

What do you get if you cross a phone with a mouthwash?

Tele-Scope.

What did the frog say when she called her boyfriend?

"Let's live hoppily ever after!"

Why did Silly Sally think she was
engaged?

*Because her boyfriend said he'd give her
a ring tonight!*

MORE PHONER GROANERS

Why does an octopus need so many phones?

So it can reach out and touch someone!

What kind of music do phones love to hear?

A symphony!

Why was the goblin's phone bill so high?

He made lots of troll calls.

How does a barber make phone calls?

He cuts them short.

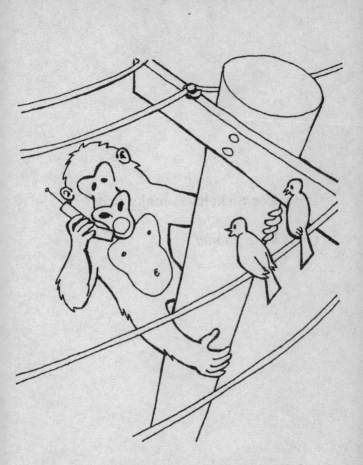

How does a baboon make phone calls?

He just monkeys around on the line!

How does a skeleton make calls?

On a bone phone!

What did the big ape say when he
dialed incorrectly?

"Oops! King Kong ring wrong."

What do you call the sound a ghost
makes when he calls you?

A phone moan.

Receptionist: Hello? Dr. Sickman's office. May I help you?

Caller: Yes! I feel funny. What should I do?

Receptionist: Try to get on television.

A psychiatrist was testing the mentality of a patient.

"Do you ever hear voices without being able to tell who is speaking or where the voices are coming from?" asked the psychiatrist.

"As a matter of fact, I do," said the patient.

"And when does this happen?" asked the psychiatrist.

"Oh," said the patient, "when I answer the telephone."